Just Be His

Joel Backstrom, B.A., M.Div., M.Ed

WESTBOW
PRESS®
A DIVISION OF THOMAS NELSON
& ZONDERVAN

WestBow Press books may be ordered through booksellers or by contacting:

WestBow Press
A Division of Thomas Nelson & Zondervan
1663 Liberty Drive
Bloomington, IN 47403
www.westbowpress.com
844-714-3454

ISBN: 978-1-6642-3172-6 (sc)
ISBN: 978-1-6642-3171-9 (e)

Print information available on the last page.

WestBow Press rev. date: 04/27/2021

I dedicate this book to my mother, Margaret Backstrom.
For many decades she has demonstrated
a quiet, confident perseverance
in her walk with Christ that has inspired all who know her.

Contents

Foreword

Any of us who have been Christian for a significant period of time have run into those fellow Christians who seem to live life on a higher plane than we have ever felt capable of. They are not only active in their external faithlife and authentically deep in their devotional habits, but also seem to exude a special godly sort of quiet, confident, perseverant aura as well. We like being around such people; in fact, in your own mind, you are probably enjoying a memory of such a person right now. They seem to emanate a profound contentedness with what God is doing in, through, and around them that we would love to emulate - but we can't seem to get there. Why not? What are we missing?

In this book I will seek to address that seemingly missing component. I hope to do so using a two-prong approach. The first two chapters will serve as a reminder to us that, as Christians, we are all dearly loved possessions of God and will explore what that actually means and doesn't mean. In the remaining chapters, I will seek, with the help of Jesus Christ and His Word, to emphasize the importance of learning how to more fully "just be His". My prayer is that the reading of this book will, by the grace of God, enable each reader to discover a more consistent and reliable

Christ-centered foundation upon which the Holy Spirit can more effectively produce the quiet, confident perseverance that we've seen in others and longed to partake of in our own hearts and souls.

Introduction

If you are a born-again Christian, you are a possession of God! The Bible makes that fact abundantly clear. In 1 Corinthians 6:19-20, the Apostle Paul tells us: **"Do you not know that your body is a temple of the Holy Spirit, who is in you, whom you have received from God? YOU ARE NOT YOUR OWN; YOU WERE BOUGHT AT A PRICE".** One chapter later (7:23) he repeats himself: **"YOU WERE BOUGHT AT A PRICE".** Several other scriptures give us that exact same message – that as a forgiven and born-again Christian, you truly belong to God, lock, stock, and barrel! In that light it would seem obvious that, if we are His possessions, our lives will reflect that truth at some level. Hopefully this book will help you to come to terms with this truth at a significantly deeper personal level than what you've already understood it to be.

With a title like "Just Be His" it is clearly possible to take two very different approaches to the subject of at hand. One way to go would be to take an exhortational tone; in essence saying, "You are His – So act like it!" I am going to do my best to avoid that tone. A confrontational approach is not as likely to have a lasting impact as an approach that is more invitational in nature. So, I've chosen to take a tone that is much more invitational.

Students of the English language would tell me that "Just Be His" is an imperative clause and therefore by nature a somewhat admonitory or confrontational statement. Yes, it is an imperative clause, but, in this case, I don't intend that it be taken in any sort of confrontational manner at all. My Greek professor used to remind us often that many of the scriptural imperatives such as "Repent and be baptized every one of you" (Acts 2:38), or, "Believe in the Lord Jesus and you will be saved" (Acts 16:31), or, "Come to Me all you who are weary and burdened" (Matthew 11:28) are in actuality literary devices called "Gospel imperatives". In other words, they are indeed commands but they are issued in gospel form as a gracious invitation to us, meant for our good, by a loving God who wants us to receive the Gospel good news of the abundant life available to us as His possessions in Christ. That is the sense in which I hope you will understand the phrase "Just Be His".

As a way of narrowing the focus of the discussion, consider this. The Christian life has been presented by some Bible scholars as consisting of three equally important components all working together, but at varying intensities, to produce a balanced, Christ-honoring, Christ-like lifestyle. Those three components could be labeled as follows: (1) A holy activism; (2) A restless searching for depth; and, (3) A quiet, confident perseverance, or what Eugene Peterson has called "a long obedience in the same direction". Which of these components is most evident at any given time in a Christian's life is dependent upon several things including one's maturity in the faith, one's present circumstances, even perhaps one's age, but, of course, most influential of all in this determination is the will of God for that person at that point in time as it is inspired, revealed, and encouraged by the Holy Spirit in the life and circumstances of that person's life.

This book is intended to provide some understanding of, and underpinning for, the third component mentioned above, that being the quiet, confident perseverance that we see and reverence in the lives of many of our Christian forebears and mentors. Of the three, it is often the least referenced in popular preaching and teaching. We are constantly urged toward lives that demonstrate a holy activism, and we certainly know intuitively the value of pursuing a deeper walk with Christ and His Word, yet without the third component, the quiet, confident, steadfast perseverance of a settled faith, the Christian life is to some degree unbalanced or incomplete, perhaps less rich than it could be. It is my contention that this kind of quiet, confident perseverance is most readily found in the true recognition and convinced acknowledgement of the fact that as a born again Christian I am completely and continuously a treasured possession of God - the assured conviction that I am His.

This state of being is more than just the achievement of a degree of peace or restfulness in this life because that would leave out the perseverance or steadfastness aspect that is necessarily involved here. It is also more than just perseverance or steadfastness alone because teeth-gritting persistence will always break down at some point unless there is a foundational quiet confidence backing it -which only a recognition of the grace and love of Christ, our

Creator and Redeemer, can supply. When a person truly recognizes and knows without a doubt, down in the deepest recesses of their heart and soul, that it is true that they are a forever beloved and prized possession of the Almighty God and Lord of the universe, and if they choose to "live out" that knowledge, it is not only possible that they will find a quiet, confident, and settled perseverance in living out the Christian life, it is almost a certainty.

Completing this thought, Ole Hallesby, noted Norwegian theologian of the early to mid 20th century, says of this component of Christian living, "Nothing is so blessed to the soul as this quiet, unceasing fellowship with the Lord…[it] exceeds all else that we can experience of peace and joy, inner satisfaction and security." (God's Word For Today, Augsburg Fortress, 1994). It is my sincere hope that this book will be useful to you, and to the work of the Holy Spirit within you, as you seek to explore and appropriate this component more fully in the context of your own Christian life.

NOTES

Chapter 1

You Are His – Part One: What Being A Possession Of Christ Means

Ephesians 2:10: We are God's workmanship, created in Christ Jesus to do good works, which God prepared in advance for us to do.

Romans 6:17-18: But thanks be to God that, though you used to be slaves to sin, you wholeheartedly obeyed the form of teaching to which you were entrusted. You have been set free from sin and have become slaves of righteousness.

Before we launch into a discussion about what it means to "just be His", we will first lay out the foundational groundwork of what it means to belong to God in the first place, what being His means on a factual level, as well as what it does not mean.

If you are at all familiar with the Scriptures you know that there are several biblical motifs that relate to the relationship between Jesus Christ and the Christian (or His Church). Here are a few of them: Head and body, Vine and branches, Father and prodigal, Father and child, Shepherd and sheep. Also among these motifs but not often referred to in recent decades, at least in western societies, is the motif of Owner and possessions. In western cultures most people are at least somewhat resistant to the idea of being owned by anyone. Even we who claim to be Christians have trouble with this even though we know, at least intellectually, that only as possessions of Christ will we ever be able to find true freedom in this earthly life to be followed by eternal life in heaven. Why are we so often resistant to the idea of ownership by Christ? Because in most of our societies we have all been deceived into believing the idea that we as individuals are fully self-empowering, quite capable of self-sufficiency and independence.

In recent times belief in this idea of a self-empowered existence has been rendered much harder, if not impossible, to swallow. Let me explain. I write these words in the second half of the year 2020, a year in which the whole world has been rocked by the advent of the deadly coronavirus known as Covid-19, most national economies have gone haywire, and multiple countries all around the globe, including the USA, have seen unprecedented civil unrest, protest, and violence. A world that had once seemed quite manageable and orderly has now shown itself to be chaotic and totally unpredictable. Many, even in Christian circles, are feeling quite disoriented, if not completely lost in this new and strange world. In this moment in time, the biblical motif of Owner and possessions is suddenly much more palatable, and is in fact able to provide great comfort at least to those of us who call ourselves Christians, because we are, IN NO WAY, lacking direction, or lost, or drifting – at least not as far as our God and Savior is concerned.

You see, if you are a born-again believer in Christ, then you are God's property, both created and redeemed by Him, and He likely has positioned you right where He wants you to be at all times, despite any appearances that might argue otherwise. Remember back to what we saw in I Corinthians 6:19-20: "You are not your own. You were bought with a price." Think about it. You are not your own. You belong to God. And you are where you are precisely because you belong to God. How can I say so confidently that you belong to Him? Because He bought you with a price, the unthinkable price of sending Jesus Christ, His one and only Son, to this earth to suffer and shed His blood on your behalf.

While you may rebel at the concept of being owned on a societal level, on a spiritual level you are forced to acknowledge that you are definitely owned – and that there are only two possible owners, God or Satan. The good news is that when believe in Jesus Christ as Savior and Lord of your life, the ownership of your life is transferred from the hate-filled and doomed kingdom of Satan to the eternal kingdom of our loving God, by far the best thing that could ever happen to you.

DOES IT REALLY SAY THAT?

——

Now, lest you think the concept of an Owner and possessions motif is something I've "proof-texted" using only one small section or two of scripture, let's look at the wider context of scripture for corroboration for this concept.

First of all, throughout the entire Old Testament historical setting, the faithful believers that were always found scattered throughout the not-always-faithful nation of Israel certainly saw themselves as possessions of Yahweh, their eternal and almighty God. He had made it clear to them, from the start, that they were His chosen people, a "peculiar people", set aside for His use. For these true believers it was both a comfort and a privilege to be His prized possessions.

In the New Testament, aside from the passages in the epistles to the Corinthians that I alluded to in the introduction, there are also many further allusions to the fact that we as New Testament Christians are also truly prized possessions of Jesus Christ. For now, I will quote just three examples:

1. John 10:27-28: [Jesus Himself said]: My sheep listen to My voice. I know them and they follow Me. I give them eternal life, and they shall never perish; no one can snatch them out of My hand.

2. Romans 7:4: So my brothers, you also died to the law through the body of Christ, that you might belong to Another, to Him who was raised from the dead, in order that we might bear fruit to God.

3. Titus 2:13-14: ...we wait for the blessed hope – the glorious appearing of our great God and Savior, Jesus Christ, who gave Himself for us to redeem us from all wickedness and to purify for Himself a people that are His very own, eager to do what is good.

Another indication of the appropriateness of using the Owner and possessions motif is the frequent and liberal use of references to Christ as our redeemer. A redeemer, by definition, is one who ransoms or buys back property or possessions which once were his. The implication in numerous New Testament references is clearly obvious – that Christ is the purchaser and we are the re-possessed property. Just a few scripture references that definitively refer to Christ as our Redeemer, which I will leave for you to verify on your own, are Ephesians 1:13-14, Colossians 1:13-14, and First Peter 1:18-19.

One last, but more subtle corroboration of the Owner and possessions motif as a valid concept in the interpretation of the New Testament is the repeated reference by most of the apostolic writers of the New Testament to themselves as the "doulos" of God or of Jesus Christ. "Doulos" is a Greek word that we generally see translated as "servant", and rightfully so. But we must also bear in mind that the apostles wrote their words in the context of the Roman Empire, and in that context, a servant was nothing more than a piece of property, owned by his or her master, and completely at the mercy and disposal of the master, for better or worse. Thus, the apostolic writers labeled themselves as possessions of God or of Jesus Christ – and were joyful and happy to do so. From their perspective, there was no better position to be in than to be the property of the God who gave His own Son to redeem them and give them new life for now and for all eternity. Some examples for several of the apostles are as follows: For Paul, see Romans 1:1, Philippians 1:1, and Titus 1:1; for Peter, see 2 Peter 1:1; for John, see Revelations 1:1; for James, see James 1:1; and for Jude, see Jude 1:1.

Love, Renovation, Purpose

Having established the validity of the Owner and possessions motif in the Bible, let us move on to the prospects that this gives us as believers in Jesus Christ. What does it really mean for you to be a possession of God in Christ?

[1.] First and foremost, being a possession of God in Christ means that you are dearly loved by God. He created you and then bought you back with His own blood in the person of Jesus Christ. Literally thousands of books have been written about the love of God as revealed in His works of creation and redemption. Thousands more have been written about the amazing truth that Christ now lives in us and sanctifies us through the agency of the Holy Spirit. Perhaps less remembered are God's promises that He will providentially preserve us and our planet every hour of every day, that Christ "is with us always, to the very end of the age" (Matt. 28:30), and that He "will never leave us nor forsake us" (Hebrews 13:5). After looking comprehensively at what we've just outlined, what more could God possibly do to show you that you are most certainly a much loved, valued, and wanted possession!

[2.] Second, being a possession of God in Christ means that, as would any good owner of property, God wants to maintain and renew your viability as His beloved possession, and even beyond that, He wants to make improvements on you and in you. Our Lord Jesus Christ will use the circumstances of your life – especially, it would seem, the more difficult ones - to continually and repeatedly bring you to the point of a focused self-examination that will help you identify which doors in your heart you have to this point kept closed to Him and to the cleansing work of His Holy Spirit. Then when He has led you to the identification of those areas, He will proceed to prompt you to seek His help in addressing the issues that lie behind those doors. That is one of His greatest desires for you: that as His possession you will always be open to His renewal, maintenance, and improvement projects, seeking to grow in Christlikeness and in Christian joy and peace.

[3.] Third, being a possession of God in Christ means that He surely has very definite purposes in mind for you. Even as His Spirit is moving forward with renewal and improvement processes, God will also be setting you aside for the even greater things He has in mind for you. He has designed you in such a way that He can use you to work out His eternal purposes here on earth in very unique ways. And as you continue to grow in Christlikeness via the ministry of the Word and the work of the Holy Spirit, you will, as time goes on, do His will and work in an increasingly clear and effective manner.

Sadly, I fear that many, if not most, Christians have been misled into believing that most of the works of outreach and/or evangelism they do on God's behalf, have to be tied to, if not totally directed by, their local church and its resources. But, God's intent for you is not restricted in any such manner. His underlying purpose for you in this very moment, and in every other moment of your life, is not complicated or involved at all. He is asking you to simply **be available** to do what only you can do within the restrictions of your own personal sphere of life. JUST BE AVAILABLE – available to do the things that only you could ever have come to consider, in terms of sharing the love of Christ within the realm of your current personal world. That is all He asks – that you, by faith in Him, will always be found open to His unique callings and purposes for your life, as He makes them known to you throughout your life.

The words of Ephesians 2:10, which appeared at the beginning of this chapter, are very fitting at this point. Please feel free right now to personalize the words of this verse as they apply to you and your current situation: You, yes YOU, are God's workmanship, created in Christ Jesus to do good works, which God prepared in advance for YOU, and only YOU, to do.

So to review – what again does it mean to be a possession of God, to be truly His?

1. It means that He loves you, His workmanship, very deeply.
2. It means that He is committed to renewing and making improvements on you and in you.
3. It means that He will put you into His service in unique, fulfilling and personalized settings.

NOTES

_____

_____

_____

_____

_____

_____

_____

_____

_____

_____

_____

_____

_____

_____

_____

_____

_____

_____

_____

Chapter 2

You Are His – Part Two: What Being A Possession Of Christ Does Not Mean

Now that we've discussed briefly what it means to be a possession of Jesus Christ, let's flip that discussion on its end and think about the inverse of that concept - what it does NOT mean to be a possession of Jesus Christ. It is probable that many of you will have some misgivings about the whole idea of an Owner and possessions motif, so we will now take the time to deal with four of the potential misconceptions that often arise in the minds of those who choose to sound the depths of their standing with God.

MISCONCEPTION #1: AS A POSSESSION OF CHRIST, I WILL LOSE MY FREEDOM.

John 8:36: So if the Son sets you free, you will be free indeed!

Most people, especially in Western cultures, have a problem with thinking of themselves as a possession of any other living being of any sort. Most of us have a very strong attachment to the idea that we are largely capable of independence and consequently that we should be free to live our lives as we so choose. This often leads to the incorrect assumption that belonging to God will rob us of that freedom. Nothing could be further from the truth.

You see, although we may feel we will be most free if we stay out of the reach of God, the opposite is true. When God is not occupying His rightful position as the owner and ruler of our lives, guiding our ways from the very center of our being, we will finds ourselves completely vulnerable to the powers of sin, Satan, and self and - we'll be helplessly enslaved by sin of some sort whether or not we are fully aware of it. Without Christ, we'll never know what it means to be truly free.

True freedom is a matter of submitting ourselves to the ownership of Christ so He can then in turn set us free to be all that we were meant to be, fully enjoying all that we were created to know, be, and do. We can never find that sweet spot on our own. That's why Jesus said, "if the Son shall set you free, you will be free indeed!"

Thus the Scripture speaks of the idea of being a willing "slave to righteousness". To be a willing slave to God and to righteousness seems to be an oxymoron or contradiction in terms. But it is not. If you are not a "slave" to God, who alone can free you to be all you were meant to be, you will, without any choice or recourse, be a slave to someone or something else - with an end result that is never desirable or good.

Let these words from Romans chapter 6 speak for themselves: "We know that our old self was crucified with [Christ] so that the body of sin might be done away with, that we should no longer be slaves to sin – because anyone who has died [with Him] has been freed from sin…Thanks be to God that, though you used to be slaves to sin, you wholeheartedly obeyed the form of teaching to which you were entrusted. You have been set free from sin and have become slaves to righteousness…Now that you have been set free from sin and have become slaves to God, the benefit you reap leads to holiness, and the result is eternal life."

Wow! If being a slave to God brings holiness, which is a lifestyle revolving around Christ and bringing with it unbridled, unending, pure peace and joy for now and all eternity, then all I can say is: BRING IT ON!

MISCONCEPTION #2: As a possession of Christ, I will lose my identity.

———

John 15:15-16: [Jesus says,] I no longer call you servants, because a servant does not know his master's business. Instead I have called you friends, for everything that I learned from my Father I have made known to you. You did not choose me, but I chose you and appointed you to go and bear fruit – fruit that will last.

The misconception that if we are possessions of Christ we will lose our sense of identity is all too common - but altogether wrong! We are all victims of our own egos, valuing our ideas of unique selfhood and of our own exceptional, unduplicatable identity. And sometimes we fall into the trap of thinking that being a possession of Christ will somehow limit or deprive us of our sense of identity. This is how Satan got to Adam and Eve in the first place, enticing them to focus on their identity apart from God and to question whether or not He really was allowing them to be all that they could be. This type of faulty thinking is still probably our most dangerous vulnerability. Why? Because we all so very desperately want to be important in one way or another! We see that impulse at work in every human being on earth, beginning in earliest infancy and continuing on through all the phases of life until the very end when one's cognitive abilities are finally no longer able to continue the effort.

Well, there is nothing wrong with that impulse to gain and hold an identity - when it is properly channeled through the understanding that we are possessions of Christ, created and redeemed for a purpose far more important than anything our feeble, flawed, earthbound minds can come up with. We are important beyond our wildest imagination when we are being used as agents of His will here on earth. And it is Christ's desire that we see ourselves as very important players in the working out of His kingdom's work here below. That is why in John 15:15-16 (see above) He chose to point out that we are His friends in this work.

What an identity! As possessions of Christ, we are friends of the one true Master of the universe, called upon by Him to personally carry out His business, appointed by Him to bring forth the fruit He has identified as our portion of His eternal plan here on earth. I challenge you to name a more meaningful and significant identity than that.

MISCONCEPTION #3: AS A POSSESSION OF CHRIST, I WILL BE MISSING OUT ON SOMETHING.

———

Romans 8:32: He who did not spare His own Son, but gave Him up for us all – how will He not also, along with Him, graciously give us all [good] things?

What are all these good things that God gives to those who receive Christ as Savior and Lord? A very concise summary is found in these verses from Psalm 103.

Psalm 103:2-5; 17: Praise the Lord, O my soul, and forget not all His benefits: – Who forgives all your sins and heals all your diseases, -Who redeems your life from the pit and crowns you with love and compassion, -Who satisfies your desires with good things so that your youth is renewed like the eagle's…From everlasting to everlasting the Lord's love is with those who fear Him and His righteousness with their children's children.

Honestly, does it sound to you after reading the above verses from Psalm 103 that you'll actually be missing anything of any true importance in life if the Lord Jesus Christ is in possession of your life? I think not. And yet it is very common for people to say something to the effect that they don't want to give up control of all aspects of their lives to Christ because they're not ready to give up certain parts of their present existence. If you are such a one, what you are really saying is that you believe that if you allow yourself to belong to Christ you are going to be missing out on things that you are not willing to miss out on or leave behind.

Perhaps the feeling that you'll somehow be "missing out" has something to do with an affinity for one or more of what the Scripture calls "the desires of the sinful nature" (see Galatians 5:16-21). Sometimes even Christians want to hang on to the "freedom" to engage in such things as unrestrained "partying", or drunkenness, or immoral relationships, etc. While no one is denying that these practices can seem to be very pleasant, at least in the moment, we also know very well that the consequences of our indulgences are highly unpleasant and often have far-reaching effects upon our lives. And the most harmful effect is the estrangement from God and all His benefits that inevitably results when we continue to allow ourselves to engage in behaviors and thought patterns that are so blatantly in opposition to what God intends for us as His possessions.

Obviously, one is very shortsighted if they feel it is worth it to trade in the benefits of a relationship with Christ in order to indulge in the temporary pleasures of the "flesh". They are allowing a Satan-produced smokescreen to blind them to what is truly of the greatest benefit to them, both in the here and now - and also for all eternity.

Perhaps you are not clear as to exactly what it is that you feel you are going to miss out on if you allow yourself to be a possession of Christ. Perhaps there's just an amorphous, undefined feeling within you that there might be something coming down the pike in your future that you will not be able to take full advantage of if you allow yourself to belong fully to Christ. Here the culprit in your heart and soul is likely a misguided sense of needing to retain control of some of the corners of life yet to be revealed, of needing to maintain some semblance of independence in certain intimate aspects of your life.

We already addressed this to some extent in the discussion about the fear some have of losing their freedom if they truly belong to Christ. As was mentioned then: Only if the Son, Jesus Christ, as owner of your life, sets you free, will you ever be able to be truly free. Only He can set you free from the powers of sin, self, and Satan so that you can truly be all you were created to be with all the attendant joy that comes along with that state. You cannot find such joy if you insist on retaining control or independence in certain areas of life.

Jesus says: I have come that they (believers) may have life – and have it to the full! (John 10:10). Only He knows what your "full" life entails, and only as His possession can He fully implement it in your life. Why would you want to miss out on that for things that are secondary, temporary, and earthbound?

MISCONCEPTION #4: AS A POSSESSION OF CHRIST, I CARRY THE BULK OF THE RESPONSIBILITY FOR THE CONTINUING VITALITY OF MY RELATIONSHIP WITH GOD.

Romans 8:14-15: Those who are led by the Spirit of God are sons of God. For you did not receive a spirit of fear that makes you a slave again to fear, but you received the Spirit of sonship. And by Him we cry, "Abba, Father."

For too many of us, the word "relationship", perhaps above all else, conjures up feelings of stress or pressure. It brings to our minds images of having to do more than our part in the maintaining of the health and vitality of the various relationships in our lives. Whether the involvement be with our spouse, our parents, our children, our employer, or our friends we want to believe that each party ought to do their fair share of the relationship-building, more or less on a 50-50 basis, but often, when we perceive that not to be the case, we feel pressure to not only do our part to maintain the relationship, but to take on what we view to be even more than our share of the load.

It is all too easy to carry this line of thinking into our relationship with Christ, to make ourselves "slaves again to fear", as the Apostle Paul puts it above, making ourselves fully responsible for the health and vitality of the whole endeavor. This is a big mistake, one that robs us of much joy. Remember, our Lord and Savior Jesus Christ owns us, and since we are His much valued, beloved belongings, He is more than ready to do the lion's share of the work to keep our relationship with him vital. Yes, it is true that we must cooperate with the promptings of His Spirit within us as He reveals His plans for us, but He is the One who will carry the load. To refuse to allow Him to do so is not only harmfully draining for us, but is counterproductive to what He desires to do in our lives. More on this will follow in later chapters.

For now, let the following succession of verses speak to you on this topic:

Philippians 2:12-13: …Continue to work out your salvation with fear and trembling [or deep reverence], for it is God who works in you to will and to act according to His good purpose.

Colossians 1:10-11: We pray this in order that you may

live a life worthy of the Lord and may please Him in every way…being strengthened with all power according to His glorious might, so that you may have great endurance and patience…

2 Corinthians 12:9: [The Lord] said to me, "My grace is sufficient for you, for my power is made perfect in weakness." Therefore I will boast all the more gladly about my weaknesses, so that Christ's power may rest on me.

It's clear from the passages above that we are not the ones who ought to be taking on the role of primary caretaker in our relationship with Christ. He desires to be that caretaker and only He has the power and resources to do it so successfully that the results last for all eternity. So take the pressure off yourself. It is not within your powers to make this happen. You belong to Him, the all-powerful God, so let Him carry the load.

NOTES

_____

_____

_____

_____

_____

_____

_____

_____

_____

_____

_____

_____

_____

_____

_____

_____

_____

_____

Chapter 3

God's Invitation: You Are His – So Just Be His

Matthew 11:29-30: [Jesus says,] Take my yoke upon you and learn from me, for I am gentle and humble in heart, and you will find rest for your souls. For my yoke is easy and my burden is light.

Clearly the operative word in the two verses quoted above is the word "yoke". To be placed under a yoke typically implies that ownership is involved and that submission is not negotiable. However, in Matthew 11:29, Jesus instructs us to willingly take His yoke of ownership upon ourselves because it is to our benefit to do so. This is another of His Gospel imperatives, thus it is a gracious invitation! Although it may seem counterintuitive and paradoxical to the human mind, He assures us that to take on His yoke is the only way to find true rest for our souls, along with the peace and joy that accompanies that rest. When we willingly submit to His ownership and guidance in our lives, only then will we find that security not otherwise available to us, a security of which we can be fully confident and in which we can persevere come what may.

In this chapter, I am calling on you to make the choice to explore the joys of "just being His", to learn to allow yourself to fall back into His loving arms where you can cultivate the quiet, confident mode of perseverance that was first mentioned way back in the introduction to this book as the third, often overlooked component of Christian life. Not that we are to forsake the other two components. Clearly, both holy activism and diligence in devotional practices are of utmost importance, but a balance of all three components is crucial, so now I will seek to persuade you to try to learn to take your foot off the gas more often, choosing instead to submit to the yoke of the gentle, humble Savior who wants you to enjoy rest in your soul, the inexplicable peace and joy that He lovingly implants within His yoking process.

Paradigm Shift

This learning to "just be His" will require an intentional paradigm shift on our part, a major shift, one that will probably have to occur repeatedly before it finally settles in to the soil of our hearts. It is deeply ingrained in most of us to believe, not so much that we belong to God and are His, but that, for the most part, we are "our own" and thus are largely "on our own" when it comes to the things of this life. Sadly, we constantly find ourselves falling victim to that lie, even in our dealings with God. Certainly within our personally prescribed times of worship and devotion we recognize that we do actually belong to God, but we quickly lose sight of that truth once we re-enter the "real world".

To correct this faulty fallback mechanism, we will have to intentionally learn and relearn, time and again, what it truly means to be His and how to fully accept the fact at a heart-and-soul level that we really do belong to Him as beloved and valuable possessions, 24/7, all day, every day.

In order to do this, let's first recall that in an earlier chapter where we discussed what it means to be a possession of God we came up with three statements of meaning: (1) it means He will always love us deeply, (2) it means He will renew and make improvements on and in us, and, (3) it means He will direct us into unique, meaningful, personalized settings for service.

All three of these statements were made in an objective and somewhat intellectually-oriented manner. They stated in a straightforward, grammatically active voice what it is that God will do as the Owner in the relationship between us. Now we will need to change the grammatical setting to a subjective, passive voice so that we can examine what it can mean to us personally to just be His – to be the beloved possessions in the Owner-possession relationship that exists between God and us – and to follow up on that on a practical level.

So – ask yourself, this time on a deeply personal level, what it could mean for you to just be His. Processing all three of the above statements of meaning on that basis, you must now honestly answer the following questions: (1) "Will I allow myself to be fully loved by God?"; (2) "Will I allow myself to be renewed and improved upon by God?"; and, (3) "Will I allow myself to be directed into His service as He see fit?".

It's tempting to just answer affirmatively to the above questions; we're conditioned to do so. But it is easier said than done. As was mentioned earlier, we tend to drift relentlessly back to thinking we're capable of handling things on our own, so it isn't necessarily natural for us to allow ourselves to let God in as Owner and Master. We will have to learn that, each time we drift away from Him, we can return to the truth, backed, of course, by favorite supporting Scriptures that reassure us: "I am His", "I belong to Him", and "He's got my back, all day, every day".

WHY THE HESITANCE?

There are some identifiable reasons for our hesitance to fully buy into the concept of "just being His" and to instead drift back and away from Him. One, as mentioned, is our natural, inborn, and ingrained conditioning to try to handle everything on our own, but we often have other issues that compound the difficulty of our situation:

Perhaps you are by nature in the melancholic category, one of those who typically "see the glass as half empty". That would make it considerably more difficult for you to acknowledge that you are capable of learning to just be His, or of acquiring the accompanying quiet, confident spirit that can always land you in a good and positive place come what may. Or it may be that you are simply anxiety-prone and have trouble putting much trust in anyone or anything at all.

Or perhaps you are one of the thousands of Christians who are overly invested in the cultural worship of "productivity" and "busyness" and have great trouble backing away from that method of maintaining a self concept you can live with. If this is true of you, then you will likely resist the idea of simply letting yourself belong to Christ and of entrusting yourself to Him. For many of us, it is very hard to set aside our own will and the desire to "do it my way". It is hard to entrust ourselves to Christ and His care and keeping, even after recognizing that as His possessions He has granted us a position of privilege far beyond what we could ever conceive of for ourselves.

Indeed, many of us are wishy-washy on this. One minute we say "Yes, I know I am His", and the next minute we are back to worrying unnecessarily about the next decision facing us, having totally forgotten about Christ altogether. We have trouble with this, all too often, not so much because we can't believe it's true that we are His, but because we *won't* believe it's true. It's just too hard to give up that false sense of control that we insist we have over the affairs of our lives.

In any case, and whatever may be the reason for our hesitance, I hope we can agree that to willingly entrust ourselves to Him fully, to learn to "just be His", and to enjoy the benefits of so doing would be an important addition to our Christian existence. Scripture is clear in pointing out the importance of accepting His invitation in this area of our lives. Beside the passage in Matthew 11 about taking on the "restful" yoke of Christ, some other examples of Scriptural Gospel imperatives that remind us to "just be His" are listed below:

Psalm 37:4-7: Delight yourself in the Lord and He will give you the desires of your heart.

Commit your way to the Lord, trust in Him, and He will do this…Be still before the Lord and wait patiently for Him; do not fret…

Psalm 46:10: Be still and know that I am God.

Psalm 130:5,7: I wait for the Lord, my soul waits, and in His word I put my hope…O Israel, put your hope in the Lord, for with the Lord is unfailing love and with Him is full redemption.

Isaiah 40:31: Those who hope in (wait upon) the Lord will renew their strength. They will soar on wings like eagles, they will run and not grow weary, they will walk and not be faint.

1 Peter 5:6-7: Humble yourselves, therefore, under God's mighty hand, that He may lift you up in due time. Cast all your anxiety on Him because He cares for you.

RELINQUISH – REMEMBER - REQUEST

As has been made crystal clear, it is very hard for many of us to "wait for Him", to "put our hope in the Lord", to "humble" ourselves and cast our anxieties on Him…, to intentionally choose to "just be His". So I want to try to offer some help in this regard in the form of three key words: Relinquish, Remember, and Request.

Relinquish: To relinquish something is simply to let it go. In the present context, it includes the biblical concepts of acknowledging our sinful "control issue", confessing and giving it over to God, and then letting it go (repentance). We will only grow in our capacity to learn to just be His and in the quiet, confident, perseverant aspect we crave in our lives if we learn to relax the white-knuckled grip we have on the reins of our lives and entrust ourselves much more fully into the hands of our merciful and gracious "Owner". May we all take to heart the words of Deuteronomy 33:27: **The eternal God is your refuge, and underneath are the everlasting arms. He will drive out your enemy before you...**

His everlasting arms are always beneath us, regardless of how much stress, discouragement, or frustration we may feel due to misgivings, missed directions, or failures we may have experienced in the other two components of our Christian life – or in life in general. We can learn to "just be His" and rest in His arms in all the times of life – but only when we are finally willing to let go.

<u>Remember:</u> In the rush and busyness of life we so quickly forget about God's gracious desire that we be more relaxed in the assurance that we are His beloved belongings - that He loves us, is renewing and improving us in ways that matter, and is working out His purposes in and through us.

A very simple way that you can help yourself remember this is to leave yourself some written reminders incorporating a favorite Scripture or two in your devotional materials or in key places around the house. Another time-tested method of remembering that we are His is to memorize some of the pertinent verses that we've referred to so that when you need them, they are right there, always fresh in your memory, ready to help you to let go and relax back into His loving arms. Don't let the simplicity of such practices cause you to discount their power and effectiveness.

<u>Request:</u> Sincere, humble prayer is obviously a very important ingredient in learning to "just be His". If we're not communicating to God regarding the difficulties we have in allowing Him to graciously own us and in allowing ourselves in turn to be fully loved by Him, we cannot expect to experience the quiet, confident perseverance that we need to maintain a balanced and joyful Christian outlook on life.

I believe that the prayerlife of a balanced, joyful Christian should include regular requests, generally made in the absence of any manifestation of specific pressing need, for the Holy Spirit to plant frequent reminders in one's daily existence of the importance of "just being His". Don't wait until you've already been overwhelmed and knocked out-of-whack before you make these requests. Instead, make it a regular part of your prayer life. I believe that if you specifically request that you be reminded frequently to "just be His", then in those times when you most need it, that request will be honored and you will not be denied the reassurance you need.

HEART, SOUL, MIND, AND STRENGTH

Another aspect of asking God for help in "just being His" has to do with the "greatest commandment", in which Jesus specified that we are to love the Lord our God with all our heart, soul, mind, and strength. To facilitate our understanding of what's truly involved here, let's first give some very basic definitions of the four terms Jesus uses: Our heart, or spirit, is the part of us meant to relate to God; our soul is our psyche, personality, and emotions; our mind is our cognitive capabilities; and our strength is our physical capabilities.

In the context of the subject matter of this book, comprehensively loving the Lord our God would also include "just being His" with all parts of ourselves - heart, soul, mind, and strength. So we would be wise to search our hearts in this regard and then request His help in these four areas – and make it as specific to our current circumstances as possible. Holding back in any of the four areas would only make it more difficult for us to be His and to experience the benefits of that reality. Perhaps a wise way to initiate "just being His" in heart, soul, mind, and strength would be to daily pray a prayer very similar to this time-honored model: **"Lord – by your Spirit, fill my mind with truth, my soul with peace, my body with strength, and my heart with love…Amen"**

God, our Owner, clearly wants us to enjoy an life of balance, joy, and effectiveness in His service. Therefore, we can rest assured that, with the help of His Word and Spirit, we will indeed find the quiet, confident, consistent, perseverance that we'll need to live a more balanced, joyful, and effective Christian life. At the same time we'll also suffer fewer and fewer lapses back into those self-focused funks of anxiety and lack of trust in Him that plagued us so often in the past. Take Him up on His invitations. Obey His Gospel imperatives with heart, soul, mind, and strength. Act on the truth that you are His - and NOT on the fallacy that you are your own. Be still and know that He is God. **Just be His.**

"I am Yours; I am Yours
I've been bought with life so precious
I am new; I'm brand new
In you, my Jesus.

I am Yours; I am Yours
You hold all my life in Your hands
And when I hear Your Spirit calling me
I will follow, yes, I'll follow
Because I'm Yours.

(Terry Clark, Maranatha! Music, 1992

NOTES

_____

_____

_____

_____

_____

_____

_____

_____

_____

_____

_____

_____

_____

_____

_____

_____

_____

_____

Chapter 4

Start By Bursting
Some Bubbles

Psalm 90:2-4, 12: Before the mountains were born or You brought forth the earth and the world, from everlasting to everlasting You are God. You turn men back to dust, saying, "Return to dust, O sons of men." For a thousand years in Your sight are like a day that has just gone by, or like a watch in the night... Teach us to number our days aright, that we may gain a heart of wisdom.

A FULLY PRESENT GOD

Perhaps before we'll ever be able to acknowledge and address our need to better learn how to "just be His" and increasingly cultivate the quiet, confident perseverance that comes with that state, we first must be reminded of a much bigger picture. In light of the bigger picture of who God is and what He's done we will perhaps be able to see more clearly the folly of thinking we can "go it on our own", and of purposely deciding against "just being His" in certain areas of life.

In Acts 17, verses 10-34, we read the story of the Apostle Paul and his visit to the city of Athens, Greece. As he travelled through the various parts of Athens, he was utterly amazed by how pagan the city was. They had a god for this – a god for that – a god for everything. And so, when given an audience with some of the leading philosophers of the city, he attempted to give them an idea of who the Christian God is and what He is like.

In verse 28 we see Paul telling the Athenians: "**In Him we live and move and have our being".** He is telling them that the one God of Christianity is every **where** and is responsible for every **thing** that happens in every **place** on earth. And not only is He present everywhere – He is <u>fully</u> present everywhere. All of Him is there wherever you are – and not just a part of Him, and not just part of the time. "In Him we live and move and have our being", and that's 24/7.

As Christians we know that God also goes even a step farther in sharing His presence with those of us who've received His Son Jesus as Savior. Scripture makes it clear that, once we've placed our faith in Christ, God then miraculously and graciously makes it possible for Christ Himself to "live in us" and for us to "live in Him" - by virtue of said faith in Christ. In other words, if God has His way with us, we will be totally immersed by His presence! Not only will He be around us but He'll also live within us. (And as part of the package, we'll also be in Him). It's that state of being that we were intended to occupy all along, and it is a state of unlimited joy, peace, and love.

BUBBLES OF INDEPENDENCE

And yet, all too often we find ourselves opting out of this blessed state that God has made available to us. The big question is: Why would we choose to do such a thing? Sadly, at various points in life, with any one of many ill-advised rationales, we decide, perhaps initially without conscious intent, to create what I will call "bubbles of independence" that we then purposefully try to keep Him from entering and occupying. In light of who God is, the "why" of such choices defies all explanation, other than to acknowledge the cunning deceitfulness of Satan's influence in this world – as well as the depths to which our own sinful nature and human depravity can sink.

These "bubbles of independence" that we try to maintain are always – always – sourced in our own ego and self-focus. We stubbornly refuse to believe that God knows better than us, so we sinfully try to create bubbles where we are in control. Common bubbles of independence might include the following: insisting that we can take care of our own problems in our own way and time without bringing it to God in prayer; pridefully trying to ride herd over ridiculous amounts of self-glorifying "busy-ness" in order to maintain an image; or purposely attempting to hide what we know to be flagrant sin. But, of course, the number of possibilities is as numerous as the number of believers in the world.

You have your bubbles of independence - I have mine. Perhaps now is the time to own up to that - and then by

God's grace may He show us how ridiculous it is for us to be trying to float those bubbles of sin in His presence. I will try to help matters by giving you a far-fetched illustration of the level of foolishness actually involved in our insistence on hanging on to our bubbles.

Imagine a fish in the very middle of the vast Pacific Ocean, thousands of miles from any landform. This fish, being smarter than the average fish, realizes that, isolated way out there in the Pacific, it is totally dependent on the ocean for oxygen, food, and movement, but for some reason it decides it needs to maintain some degree of independence from mother ocean. So, simply because it can, it creates a bubble around itself. It adds features that allow oxygen to diffuse into the bubble from the surrounding water, that enable it to encapsulate food and bring it in through the bubble walls, and that allow it to steer its way around by a mechanism attached to its tail. And so, it pridefully floats around in its little niche of the vast Pacific.

A ridiculous concept isn't it? For whether this egotistical fish gets it or not, it is still totally dependent on the ocean around it for oxygen, food, and movement. The fish has simply complicated things by all its strivings.

You get the picture I'm sure. We as Christians do a very similar thing in our relationships with God when we refuse to be His and to put everything in His hands. Think about it…We belong to Him! He created us and then He bought us back from sin and Satan with the blood of His very own beloved Son Jesus. Isn't it time we burst our bubbles of independence and just let ourselves be His today? He alone knows what is best for us in every area of life - and He greatly desires to be involved in it all.

Why not take the time to identify those resistant bubbles of independence in your life and ask your Savior and Owner to help you bring them in line with His will? He will surely answer that prayer! Colossians 3:15 gives us this Gospel imperative: "Let the peace of Christ rule in your hearts". The clear implication is that this is a conscious choice; it is a choice we begin to pursue when we intentionally choose against maintaining our bubbles of independence and instead choose to let ourselves "just be His".

NOTES

_____

_____

_____

_____

_____

_____

_____

_____

_____

_____

_____

_____

_____

_____

_____

_____

_____

_____

_____

_____

Chapter 5

How's Your Aroma?

2 Corinthians 2:14-15: But thanks be to God, who always leads us in triumphal procession in Christ and through us spreads everywhere the fragrance of the knowledge of Him. For we are to God the aroma of Christ among those who are being saved and those who are perishing.

In literature and motion pictures we often encounter the heart-wrenching scene of a grieving person who has recently lost a loved one entering into the room of that loved one, seeking out an article of clothing that belonged to that loved one, and then burying their face in that article of clothing in order to take in the aroma of that now departed loved one. Indeed, it is said that each of us actually does have our own unique scent or aroma, thus it makes sense that our aroma would remain in an article of clothing for quite some time after we last wore it.

The aroma of Christ

The Apostle Paul says in the passage from Corinthians quoted above that "we are to God the aroma of Christ among those who are being saved and those who are perishing". How does it happen that we come to carry the aroma of Christ? As hard as this may be to comprehend, Scripture assures us that it is true, that we, as possessions of Christ, are indeed "clothed with Christ". And if we are clothed with Christ, then it follows that we will carry the aroma of Christ wherever we go. We are His aromatic clothing! But it would also appear that we are just as likely to be unaware that we are carrying the supernatural aroma of Christ as we generally are to the fact that we are carrying our own unique, natural, human aroma. So, let me provide two supporting Scripture passages for the amazing truth that we truly are clothed in Christ if by faith we belong to Him:

> **Galatians 3:27: You are all sons of God through faith in Christ Jesus, for all of you who were baptized into Christ have clothed yourselves with Christ.**

> **Romans 13:12,14: So let us put aside the deeds of darkness and put on the armor of light… Rather, clothe yourselves with the Lord Jesus Christ.**

Diminishing the aroma

While all this is amazingly true due solely to the grace and love of God for us as revealed in the person and work of Jesus Christ, it is also sadly true that, despite being clothed with Christ, we sometimes cause His aroma to be diminished or deflected. We do this when we, subtly and likely unknowingly, try to separate ourselves from Christ, who is of course the source of the aroma. It happens when, as previously discussed, we enter those periods of life when we are not allowing ourselves to "just be His", usually when we are trying too hard to live for Jesus and serve Him in the power of the flesh. By way of illustration, let me tell you some of my own story:

After completing college and student teaching, I first worked for ten-plus years to get established as a public high school teacher. Then the Lord put a new calling on my life and I spent the next 25 years in various aspects of vocational Christian service - completing seminary while teaching at a Christian school, serving as a parish pastor, becoming an Army National Guard chaplain, and returning again to a Christian school setting as a teacher and administrator. Finally, I spent the last eight years of my 44-year working life back in a public high school classroom.

Truthfully speaking, as I look back on all those years, I now realize that for more than half of that time I was not a very "aromatic" Christian. Yes, I certainly did know that, having received Christ as my Savior, I belonged to God and that, as His possession, He was preparing me for and sending me into the various callings He had in mind for me in life. And I also know that He did use me in His service to help others become His and draw near to Him - but I'm afraid it was often the case that, while He was able to use me, it was frequently in spite of myself. Yes, I was spreading the aroma of Christ in my wake, but I see now that it was likely diminished because, all too often, I looked at life as if I was my own, not His, and I acted accordingly. Too often I internalized and let myself believe the mistaken notion that it was all up to me to make things happen and to create "fragrant" openings for the Lord to move into. Intellectually, I knew better, but at heart-level I wasn't quite ready to accept the restful yoke of Christ and let myself simply be His, allowing His "living water" to flow into me and through me and His life-changing aroma to flow out of me, without feeling it was up to me to get out in front of Him and "run interference" for Him. I was trying too hard to serve Christ in the power of my own flesh.

Because of the artificiality that comes out of that kind of mistaken self-dependence I was clearly not as effective as I might have been had I been more accepting of the fact that He is my gracious and loving Owner and that He earnestly desires to lead me by the hand on the best path through every situation that I encounter. I wish I'd recognized this at a deeper heart-level than I did, that I'd somehow been more strongly urged to learn to "just be His" – but now, a little wiser for the wear, I'm telling you about it and I'm strongly urging you: for your own sake and for the sake of those who are a part of your world, please recognize the powerful fact that simply because you belong to Christ you always carry with you His fragrant, life-changing aroma! Use the fact that you are His, clothed in Him, and thus carrying His aroma, to then spread His aroma –without applying the copious amounts of self-importance and self-dependence that we so often feel we need to bring to bear in our encounters with others.

An interesting comparison can be made at this point. In Matthew 5:13-16, Jesus says that we as His disciples are the "salt of the earth" and the "light of the world". In Second Corinthians 2:15, the Apostle Paul says that we are the "aroma of Christ". What new insight could Paul possibly seek to add to the picture by saying this? I don't claim to have the answer to that. But as a former chemistry and physics instructor I can offer a hypothesis for your consideration.

In the heat of an anxious moment, we Christians can, if we so choose, neutralize our saltiness or douse our light - at will. And Jesus implies in Matthew 5 that, sadly, this does happen. An aroma, on the other hand, is not so easily dispensed with. An aroma tends to linger wherever you have been, even when you are not aware of it and even when you perhaps would rather it didn't. One way of looking at this is to let the salt and light represent the things we do and say in our Christian witness, which can of course be easily suppressed if we so desire – while the aroma represents who we are, incorporating the reality that Christ is in us and we in Him, which is not such an easily suppressible phenomenon.

This is both exciting and sobering. It is exciting because it tells us that Christ's ownership of us and His presence in us will be evident even when we are not aware of it. It is sobering for the same reason. If we are the aroma of Christ and we are not aware of it, we can all too easily diminish or even corrupt His aroma, like I did, by relying too much on the vision and power of our own human flesh.

No sitting back

A disclaimer once again needs to be made at this point. I am by no means advocating a wimpy, "let go and let God" type of spirituality, where we sit back and do nothing, expecting that God will take care of everything Himself. He could do that, but He chooses not to. Instead, He has appointed us to be His ambassadors and agents here on earth. And we are to do this by employing a wise and strong faith in our Owner and Master, a faith that seeks a proper balance that lies somewhere between a weak, infantile irresponsibility and an "I'm in charge", self-focused overconfidence. We are well-advised to once again recall and mentally adjust to the very important message of Ephesians 2:10 that "we are God's workmanship, created in Christ Jesus to do good works, which God prepared in advance for us to do". This means we remain always available to God, ready to do the best we can with the opportunities He places before us, but, having done so, ready then also to leave it in His capable hands. We must stop imagining that we are the ones who have to "move all the pieces".

Remember always, that, by faith, you are clothed in Christ and thus you are His aromatic clothing, bringing with you everywhere you go the presence of a loving and gracious Owner and Lord, one who is "gentle and humble in heart" to the point of being willing to redeem His possessions by the sacrifice of His own precious blood. Philippians 4:5 tells us: "let your gentleness be evident to all" and implies that this provides to others the clue that the gentle and humble "Christ is near". In this way, the aroma of Christ will often provide you with God-given opportunities, good works He has prepared in advance for you, which will help others as well to "just be His".

NOTES

_____

_____

_____

_____

_____

_____

_____

_____

_____

_____

_____

_____

_____

_____

_____

_____

_____

_____

_____

Chapter 6

Reclaiming His Own: Prodigals, Doubters, Despondents

Romans 8:35-39: Who shall separate us from the love of Christ? Shall trouble or hardship or persecution or famine or nakedness or danger or sword?...No, in all these things we are more than conquerors through Him who loved us... nor will anything else in all creation be able to separate us from the love of God that is in Christ Jesus our Lord.

Having spent all of my childhood and many of my adult years in central and western North Dakota, a very specialized image comes to my mind when I hear the word "reclamation project". This image is that of gigantic "open pit" lignite coal mines encompassing massive acreages, perhaps hundreds of acres each. Over time I also became aware of the massive time periods involved - from the time when the land is first leased from the farmer or rancher to be taken out of production for mining to the time when that same land is finally "reclaimed" to the point where it is "as good or better" than it was before it was ever mined, and is ready to be put back into production as farmland or ranchland once again.

I also have come to recognize that we Christians are, from time to time, also best classified as reclamation projects – God's reclamation projects. Unlike the leasing farmers and ranchers in the example of the lignite coal mines, God never relinquishes His ownership of those of us who belong to Him in Christ. As we saw in the Romans passage above, nothing can cause Him to set aside His possessions - but He does allow us to exercise free will in our decision-making in our roles as His property. Unfortunately, this means we sometimes make decisions that cause us to slide from the positions He graciously desires for us to occupy as His possessions. These periodic episodes of self-imposed exile from His best for us will inevitably bring about feelings of being separated from God and, in the process, we will lose any sense of "just being His" or of resting in His everlasting arms.

However, since God never for a second moves from His position of loving Owner but continues, as always, to try to draw us near, we can rest assured that He will do whatever is necessary to "reclaim" us and bring us back to the place of blessedness and fruitfulness that He has in mind for us. Jesus promises us in John 10:28-30: "I give [my sheep] eternal life, and they shall never perish; no one can snatch them out of My hand. My Father, who has given them to Me, is greater than all; no one can snatch them out of my Father's hand. I and the Father are one".

That being the case, let's now take an honest look at three roles we frequently slip into that cause us to slide out of the positions of favor that God our Owner desires for us. And then, finally, let's discuss what can be done, with His grace and help, to decrease the frequency of these slides.

Prodigals, doubters, and despondents

The three roles we all too often find ourselves assuming as Christians, despite being owned and lovingly cared for by our God, are those of prodigal, doubter, and/or despondent. Remember, we are not talking about unbelievers here but about Christians who are, for various reasons, sliding out of God's purposes for them, sometimes seeming to be trying purposely to jump out of the arms of their gracious Master.

Prodigals: A prodigal is a person who by definition is given over to irresponsibility or dissipation. While we all likely know of at least one prodigal in our family or congregation, we don't usually think of ourselves as being in that category. The truth is that we periodically do fall into the role of a prodigal. In his book, A Shepherd Looks At Psalm 23, W. Philip Keller, while discussing verse 3 ("He restores my soul"), identifies three precipitating factors that lead us to be prodigal and in need of God's restoration. They are self-indulgence, self-assertion, and self-assurance. We are all vulnerable to each of the three.

Self-indulgence might be associated with the word "libertinism" and reflects a sinful attitude that recklessly states "I want no restraints placed on me with respect to this aspect of my lifestyle". Self-assertion in more current terms might be called "entitlement" and reflects the all-too-common idea that "I and my individual rights always come first". Self-assurance is simply another way of saying "arrogance" and reflects the prideful elevation of one's own capabilities and the boastful claim "I've got this" with regard to life's challenges. Are we as Christians vulnerable to these sinful attitudes? Indeed we are! And when they come up in our conscious thoughts we typically are already perfectly aware that they are sinful in nature, and yet we still fall victim to them periodically.

A prime example of a prodigal is the biblical Old Testament character Jonah. There is no doubt that Jonah was a believer in God. God would have never called on Jonah to preach for Him in Nineveh if he had not been a believer. And Jonah was very aware of the fact that he was sliding out of God's will when he took off for Tarshish. In Jonah 1:1, we read that he "ran away from the Lord" and in 1:10 we read that the sailors "knew he was running away from the Lord, because he had already told them so". This was a premeditated, intentional action that, in his heart of hearts, he knew would bring about unpleasant consequences. In true form of a prodigal, he did it anyway. And we all know what happened. Fortunately, he was brought to repentance via the God-ordained means of a storm and a large fish. In like manner, God will never fail to do whatever it takes to bring us, His possessions, back in line with His will so that we are once again in a position to "just be His".

Doubters: Doubters, for our purposes, are those Christians who choose to dwell on their doubts and questions beyond all justifiable need to do so. Now I know that the word "doubt" creates considerable discomfort for some of you because it seems to impart such a heavy weight of gravity and condemnation that you have trouble relating it to your own case. If so, for you, perhaps the word "faithlessness" is a better, more relatable term. In any case, doubt, or faithlessness, includes those episodes during which we have trouble believing that God or Christ and their purported love for us is actually "for real" in our present context.

Certainly, all of us have seasons of doubt that occupy our minds, probably even on a somewhat frequent basis. Such episodes, some brief and some not so brief, are normal occurrences in the life of a Christian, and they are usually beneficial in the long run, because they generally cause us to look to the Bible or other believers to try to come up with answers. In other word, most often, living through a period of doubt is actually a faith-building exercise.

But sometimes, in what amounts to a mild form of egotistical defiance, we choose to hold onto the doubt and to challenge God and those around us to provide a definitive, unequivocal solution, even though, deep down, we know that a final solution to this particular problem is likely never to appear in this present world. This is dangerous because it can morph into a nasty cynicism or even, further down the road, into a vacillating agnosticism. Once again, this is usually an intentional behavior on our part; we know we are heading down a dangerous path – but we do it anyway. It's almost as if we're trying to jump out of the hand of God.

The classic case of this is the Apostle Thomas. He doubted the authenticity and deity of Christ by refusing to believe that He had risen from the dead as He had said He would and, furthermore, this was not a momentary doubt. It lasted for at least a week according to the biblical account, and probably longer than that in actuality, but the good news is that, once again, God, through the appearances of Christ, did what was needed to bring Thomas back into his proper position as a beloved and valuable possession of God. The amazing end result of this was that Thomas went on to become known as the "apostle to India" where he eventually gave his life as a martyr for the cause of Christ. And God will most assuredly do the same for us. He will do what is necessary, although it may take some time, to reassure us of His reality and sufficiency, doubts notwithstanding, and will unceasingly seek to convince us to return as His precious belongings to a full and certain knowledge that we are truly His.

Despondents: Despondent Christians are those who find themselves mired in low spirits due to a loss of hope, confidence, or courage. Despondency can cover a whole range of conditions - from simple discouragement to utter despair. It is important to note right at the outset that not all conditions which at first glance appear to be forms of despondency are actually associated with sinful attitudes or behaviors. Some examples are: (1) behaviors caused by organic, medical, or pathological disorders or diseases such as post traumatic stress disorder [ptsd] or bipolar disease; (2) dispiriting effects brought on by the painful but completely normal and restorative process of grieving; and, (3) lowered spirits due to the senescent decline associated with aging. All of these conditions look very much like despondency, but are not usually linked to sinful attitudes or conduct.

With that information in mind, for the purposes of our present discussion, we will be referring only to those cases that actually are associated with a degree of sinfulness, cases in which we are guilty of allowing ourselves to dwell in some form of despondency and choosing to "fester" there for long periods of time, feeling very sorry for ourselves, far removed from the position where God would have us to be.

All too easily we go from appropriate grief or concern over a situation to inappropriate self-pity and from there we inevitably begin to sink into a self-focused funk. Somewhere along the line a sinful attitude gains the upper hand and, for some reason, we tend to want to wallow in it – to varying depths and for varying times. Thus we have the fore-mentioned varying levels of despondency ranging from simple discouragement to total, disabling despair.

The biblical character that comes to mind here is Elijah. He had just come from Mount Carmel where, with God's help, he had triumphed over the evil Baal-worshipping priests employed by the royal family. Within hours, we find Elijah holed up in the desert wallowing in despondency and self-pity, asserting that no one understood or supported him and that he was all alone in his belief in God. It was obvious that, deep down, he couldn't really have believed this, for God was right there with Him all along, physically providing for Him via the ministry of an angel. But God went even one step further and certified to Elijah that "I reserve seven thousand in Israel – all whose knees have not bowed down to Baal". In other word, there was no excuse for Elijah to wallow in despondency. He simply needed, first of all, to rest after the huge drama of Mount Carmel, then to relinquish his fears to God, remember His promises, and request His guidance going forward - which Elijah did.

I myself, as a precocious pre-teen who could see very little positive in my 1960's world, had a lot of trouble with despondency. My father wisely directed me to various promises in the Scriptures, but emphasized Philippians 4:4, a Gospel imperative which instructs us to "rejoice in the Lord always". He pointed out first of all that we as Christians are to rejoice in the things of the Lord, not in what the world around us offers or does not offer. Then he followed up by reminding me that this rejoicing in the Lord is an imperative that I can choose either to heed or to ignore. In other words, rejoicing in the Lord, as well as its inverse, wallowing in despondency, are both choices I as a Christian make voluntarily. Last, as a way of correcting my misdirected thinking, he directed my attention to the last few words of the very next verse, Philippians 4:5, where it simply states "the Lord is near". He always stands right beside us, ready to help us get back into a place of awareness that we are His beloved belongings with access to all the benefits that He graciously provides (Psalm 103).

I know it's not always such a simple thing to do, but like Elijah we as Christians can choose to leave our despondencies behind us just as he did. God will surely be there to enable us, via His Word and Spirit, to again fully recognize the position of privilege He has in mind for us as His possessions. We need only to relinquish our fears and anxieties to Him, remember His promises of love and grace, and daily request His help in coming to the full assurance that we can truly "just be His" and that He will insure that all is well.

It Doesn't Have To Be This Way

Perhaps it seems to you at this point that we are doomed to a continuing series of falls into the traps of prodigality, doubt, or despondency. I am here to assure you that this is not the case! We are not helplessly vulnerable to the clutches of these disruptive attitudes and behaviors. Thanks be to God that with the help of the indwelling Christ and His Spirit, we can combat and defeat these traps much of the time. Certainly, in our own strength alone, we would fall victim to them most of the time, but as God's beloved possessions, He will always seek to remind us that we are His, and that if we will "just be His", He will supply both the strength and the resources to stay out of the clutches of sin and evil of this or any other sort.

However, if we truly desire to stay clear of the traps of prodigality, doubt, and despondency we will need to be willing to adhere to the pertinent Gospel imperatives He has laid out for us in the Scriptures. The primary Gospel imperative for us is found in Matthew 6:33 where Jesus says: "Seek first His kingdom and His righteousness, and all these things will be given to you as well". I believe "all these things" would include the strength and resources to combat the evil traps we've identified. But first, according to Jesus, we must seek His kingdom and His righteousness. How do we do that? In that regard I will mention four practices each accompanied by a standard, time-honored, secondary Gospel imperative that will help us to remain firmly assured and aware of our status as possessions of God and thus able to avoid being a constant reclamation project. Each of these practices is very familiar to us so I will comment only briefly on them, but the point here is that we do not get to just "let go and let God". As Christians we do have a part to play in our own growth and development as His possessions.

1. Take in the message of the Bible regularly. To read, hear, and/or meditate upon the Scriptures, especially the New Testament, is absolutely essential.

   II Timothy 2:15 and 3:16-17: "Do your best [study – King James Version] to present yourself to God as one who does not need to be ashamed and who correctly handles the word of truth…All Scripture is God-breathed and is useful for teaching, rebuking, correcting, and training in righteousness, so that the man of God may be thoroughly equipped for every good work".

2. Pray on an ongoing basis, or as the Apostle Paul says, "Pray continually". Don't make "rocket science" out of this. Simply mentally talk to God on an ongoing basis throughout each day, bringing to His attention the various weaknesses, uncertainties, and distresses that plague you – and don't forget to add a little thanksgiving at times as well.

   Philippians 4:6-7: "Do not be anxious about anything, but in everything, by prayer and petition, with thanksgiving, present your requests to God. And the peace of God, which transcends all understanding, will guard your hearts and your minds in Christ Jesus".

3. Spend time in communion with other Christians. This is not talking about simply showing up in a church building once a week. It means quality time spent with other Christians, often somewhere other than on church property. We are not meant to go

it alone as solo acts in a private corner of God's dominion. We are created to be social beings and this is especially important within the family of God where each and every member will frequently need some form of personalized encouragement, support, or demonstrated love from a fellow Christian.

Hebrews 10:24-25: "Let us consider how we may spur one another on toward love and good deeds. Let us not give up meeting together as some are in the habit of doing, but let us encourage one another – and all the more as you see the Day approaching".

4. Love God and others. Love, in New Testament usage, is not a touchy-feely, sentimentalized emotion. It is a pre-determined act of the will to serve God first and then others. This sort of love, agape love, is not something we can generate from our own inner human resources. Only God, via the His Holy Spirit working within us as His believing possessions, can make us capable of doing so, especially when the situation seems to be telling us that love is the last thing we need to be applying. In Him, we can love and serve even our enemies. Applying this sort of love on a regular basis goes a long way towards strengthening us against falling victim to those recurrent traps of self-focused evil that come our way.

Matthew 22:37-39: "Love the Lord your God with all your heart and with all your soul and with all your mind. This is the first and greatest commandment. And the second is like it: Love your neighbor as yourself".

If you faithfully adhere to these four Gospel imperatives, will you be totally free from the grips of the evil trio of prodigality, doubt, and despondency? No, you will continue to be assaulted by these evils all throughout your life, but the closer you adhere to these principles, the more powerful will be your ability to resist them, to the point where eventually they may become only a very minor irritation in your walk with Christ, just an occasional glitch in your continuing saga of "just being His" .

NOTES

_____

_____

_____

_____

_____

_____

_____

_____

_____

_____

_____

_____

_____

_____

_____

_____

_____

_____

_____

_____

_____

Afterword

It is so easy to lose sight of the fact that we are His and to despair of ever again "just being His". For those times when you feel yourself slipping away, I want to suggest two Scripture passages – one for your use as an individual and one for your use in family or small group settings.

For your individual use I recommend Psalm 23:
The Lord is my shepherd, I shall not be in want.
He makes me lies down in green pastures,
He leads me beside quiet waters.
He restores my soul. He guides me in paths
of righteousness for His name's sake.
Even though I walk through the valley of
the shadow of death, I will fear no evil,
For You are with me; Your rod and
Your staff they comfort me.
You prepare a table before me in the
presence of my enemies.
You anoint my head with oil; my cup overflows.
Surely goodness and love will follow
me all the days of my life,
And I will dwell in the house of the Lord forever.

For corporate use within your family or small group, I recommend Psalm 100:

Shout for joy to the Lord, all the earth.
Worship the Lord with gladness; come
before Him with joyful songs.
Know that the Lord is God. It is He
who made us, and we are His.
We are His people, the sheep of His pasture.
Enter His gates with thanksgiving
and His courts with praise;
Give thanks to Him and praise His name.
For the Lord is good and His love endures forever;
His faithfulness continues through all generations.

Bibliography

Barna, George. *Maximum Faith: Live Like Jesus.* New York: SGG Publishing, 2011.

Hallesby, Ole. *God's Word For Today.* Minneapolis: Augsburg Fortress, 1994.

Keller, W. Phillip. *A Shepherd Looks At Psalm 23.* Grand Rapids: Zondervan, 1970.

Peterson, Eugene. *A Long Obedience In The Same Direction.* Madison: Intervarsity Press, 1980.